Family Drives

Family Drives

Leland Kinsey

The New England Press
Shelburne, Vermont

ISBN 1-881535-07-X
Library of Congress Catalog Card Number: 93-71953

For additional copies of this book or for a catalog of our other
New England titles, please write:

The New England Press
P.O. Box 575
Shelburne, VT 05482

Table of Contents

I

II

I

Blessed Rooms

If, after we have made love
for one more time,
many of the places we've made love
before come to mind —
dark panelled rooms
in relatives' old houses;
light filled sea rooms
in cheap cottages;
fields, damp in spring,
overgrown in summer,
dry in fall, backs wet
or grass stained or scratched;
the cliff you leaned against
and I stood, high, sheer, and held;
by the sides of many roads
to destinations since forgotten,
the once when an old couple
came upon us and only smiled —
it is hard to tell if it is
happiness or sadness that echoes
in reconstructed moments
that have defined us clearly
to at least ourselves
if not the other.
Odd moments of adrenalin and wonder
like when you were a girl
and during thunderstorms
your mother would line you
and your sisters behind
her and in procession lead you
from room to room,
splashing holy water in each room
to save you all.

She told you men were like that,
pretty as the sky,
full of sudden terror.
Fear is not difficult to instill,
hard to erase
and, when you tell me,
your laughter is tinged with despair.
One more place we move toward,
through, away from,
trying to bless ourselves
and those we love
so that the structure of our lives
might shelter and contain.

Swimming Late

After days in the hay fields
when on each return to the barn
we would dip our whole heads
into the wash-up sink in the milkhouse,
but not be able to stop the dull aches
at the bases of our skulls,
when chaff would ride
up and down our backs like insects,
and the sun weighed down on us like   the sun,
after the last load that could be drawn
was drawn, no more or dew fall,
we would ride to the glacial pond,
walk down the barely visible path
and into water as cold as our origins.
My parents would usually stay nearer the edge
in order to see our bobbing heads
in the area reflecting sky.
If one of us stayed down too long
diving for stones by feel
a name would ring out softly,
"Blaine," or "Helen," or "Lee," and we would rise
and answer. A longer call
sometimes followed my father
if he swam across and stayed too long
in the opposite shore light oppressed by trees,
but we would hear his emergence back into our circles,
feel his soft wake.
We would walk back and change
beside the car. Riding home,
our bathing suits drying on the antenna,
we were almost cold
shivering in our cool feeling shirts and trousers.
We had a rule that tomorrow couldn't be mentioned,

talk instead of the stars,
of animals' eyes, of relatives and places
often long gone.

Tonight, after a long hot day
I've worked through, I say softly
"Here I am."
to no one's call,
to no one expecting an answer.

Solitary

I lay the neck across the block
And chop it off.
Watching the hen circle
Its shut-eyed head,
I remember a time I split my leg
Open to the bone.
In my father's world
I called my world
I was wounded for the first time I could remember,
The circles of fear my own,
Knowing child's tales of lockjaw, hospitals,
Almost blacking out as father carried me into the house
To soak my leg in the pantry sink.
Revived by the sting of epsom salts,
And a blue dauber coming through the rotted sill
To circle the sand soap tin
In search of mud or plaster
Or shavings of the peeled bone,
I felt paralyzed as a spider, a black widow
Stung in the season of this solitary hunter
For its earthen womb,
Death nest as intricate as I could build,
But my father held me and I did not die.
The blood trickling into the water stopped,
And father carried me upstairs.
I looked down the stairwell,
It was transformed into the mud cell,
We perched at its edge, my father the blue wasp, Chalybion,
Held me above the cache of comb-footed death,
The hourglass-dighted spiders.
In an updraft I would cast my web
To balloon away in time,
All my season.

I would fall away but father hung on tight.
Father watched but I could say nothing,
I left my words behind like spit,
A copper tarnish in the iron sink.

Swing

Running across stubble that would shred
horsehide and the balls of our feet,
my brother and I shagged flies
our father hit to us in the summer dusks.
Tiring of that he would teach us
to pitch and catch fastballs,
the slap in our gloves like the sound
of punching an ornery cow,
and the missed ones' slugs in the ribs
or head must have felt the same.
Teaching us hitting, he would say,
"Swing, swing, don't let them all go by."
The month after first-cut hay was in
we covered the one flat field
with glove, and bat, and ball
until the rowen grew too tall
and we left off for work that was work.
But those evenings after chores were done
when the grass-stained balls came hard,
we were grateful for flies that got above
the masking green, or for high sailing
fastballs, easy to see.

My father, if he had had a choice,
would have been an outfielder for the Red Sox,
whom he fell asleep listening to
on the car's front seat Sunday afternoons;
or a drummer in Glen Miller's band,
a sound he could still sometimes find
on the dial, and that he himself made
playing in local dance halls and bars.
He was a star on the diamond
for local town teams that rode roughshod

over the boy-men we watched play,
as we sat on or beside my mother
in her cotton dresses; and at night
as his drumsticks flashed under gaslights
and we fell asleep on bright rayon.
He was good with wood in his hands.
In the hayfield he told us stories as we played:
Iron Man, The Grey Ghost, Desert Fox,
Glen Miller's death in a plane, Little Napoleon,
The Gas House Gang, his bad knees that had stopped
him from going to war. His voice carried
to surrounding hills, seems to carry to me now.
Having let so much go by, from this distance
I try to bring things back:
How far did I stand from home?
How many times strike out?

The Fire

I. The Fire

Our neighbor came at midnight
And woke us to the barn in flames.
I heard my father shout, racing out
Half dressed, I went behind and watched,
Feeling the cold. The snow snapped
Beneath my feet, snapped like the blaze
He tried to pierce to save the animals
Stanchioned and penned, but the doors and windows
Flared like sunspots and he fell back.
We watched through the windows
As the hides of the bellowing animals caught.
They tried to shake the fire off
Till the heat made their bowels burst.
We covered our noses against the stench.
My father ran to get his gun, wanting to kill
The animals before the flames, but he could not see
Through the heat waves and only maimed.
We stood by, the fake dawn spread over us,
Reflected in its own clouds
That rose along the beams and currents,
Destruction spreading in this system.
We wet the house and waited
For the slow collapse,
The pull of the body's own weight
Drawing the heat and light to its center.
The black beams rumbled down,
Massed till at last not even light got out,
And we drew far back but were still
So heavy we could not pull away.

11

II. And After

In the morning the real dawn
Pushed in at the kitchen window
And fell on the floor before ascending
To a grey sky. First, wind that laid
The ashes westerly, then rain, too late.
I stayed in the house, watching my father
Get up again and again to leave
And check the smoldering remains.
He put his boots on each time without a word,
Without looking he seized at air and let it go,
Then went out into the rain.
The rain brought the last of the ash clouds down,
Each drop with a nucleus of ash.
The black scar leached so a small stream ran
Carrying food for an overgrowth of grass
And dock in spring, tissue on an old wound.
The poison caked on my father's boots
And he breathed the acrid fumes.
I was afraid when he came in
For his hands and face were marked
Like a penitent's with lye,
And were raw.

III. Rebuilding

The lumber in resin smelling stacks,
The land bulldozed, the scar increased,
We started to rebuild. Neighbors came.
We laid foundations, the slow toil,
Working the concrete in sheets and forms,
Hoping it wouldn't rain, it didn't.
The walls went up with pikes and ropes
And we felt victorious. I cut pegs
In the shadow of the wall
To fit the mortised joists and uprights.
I sat in speckled light from knotty walls
Listening to my father drive us hard.
He checked that everything was right,
A surety I could not match.
Then, once, I looked up and feared
For my father. His darkened back
Was wedged against the sky
As he parbuckled rafters for the very peak,
And I knew he would fall,
Such firm motion on a slim foothold
But it held all day and into dusk.
The dark flame that was himself burned,
Burned on the resin of its sweat.

IV. Height and Loss

New cattle, life moving,
Making demands that were gladly filled.
I helped in calving, tied the legs and pulled,
Drew out each life, my father
Showed me how to clear their faces.
Late in summer some cows got blackleg;
Laccoliths of disease rose in stinking sores,
Their skins turned black and brittle,
There was nothing we could do for them,
But it could not even raise my father to anger.
One day he got the post maul,
Methodically crushed their skulls
And had me help him drag them from the barn.
I skidded them away. As the barn
Began to eclipse the sun, my father stood
At the shadow's edge, a slumped figure,
Slough from a healing wound.

The Boy Whose Braces Stole the Show

For wonders his classmates couldn't compete
with a boy whose braces could
pick up radio broadcasts,
who could receive weather reports
and music and news from near and far.
His dentist said it was rare
but not unheard of, that it was like
a crystal set he had built as a kid
to listen to Dodger and Red Sox games.
The boy's father said you could unhook that one
and this one was damned inconvenient.
His mother said she wished it would stop,
a wish shared by his teacher
but not for the same reason.
Often in class when talking of times tables
or ancient history, the new rock and roll
would come out making suggestions
and requests that we boys and girls
were ready to follow and answer.
He couldn't be sent to the hall
for something he couldn't help
but she would ask him to shut his mouth
to muffle the sound a little
though his jaw amplified it fine.
We called him "Hi-fi,"
he wanted "Sci-fi," but a nick-name
he wanted was more generous
than we were willing to be.
Sometimes at communion unseen speakers
would talk to the priest,
or songs the church banned would begin,
but his mother would send him out.
Usually the stations were local,

old tunes and hardware ads,
but sometimes if conditions were right
fifty thousand watt stations in Indiana
or farther still would reach him,
made him seem directly a part of a large world
we despaired of ever touching in any way.
Then, just when girls were getting interested
and interesting, when he could be
his own record hop and DJ, when he could say
"This song's for you," and almost mean it
it ended, his teeth were straight,
when he opened his mouth to speak
he had to be thinking of something,
like the rest of us,
had to try to speak from the heart,
a remote enough place,
but sometimes his high tinny voice
seemed to be coming
from more distant places still.

My Father's Father

I stayed with you that spring my mother was ill.
I watched you plow and pick the fields.
Once you showed me a rock
You said was shaped like a man.
I could not see how the huge shape you lifted for me
Looked like a man and I made fun of it and hid.
In the afternoon I searched the attic,
The jumbled years, and sometimes I saw you
Through the window. I wanted to tell you
The rock was a man, but I stayed,
Finding mucilage pots, a butter press,
And to my great great grandmother
A letter from Scotland dated 1910.
When I opened it a sprig of heather fell,
Dry pieces scattering on the floor
Amid thousands of flies dead
From the winter sun and cold.
I read the letter in the window light.
An evening wind rattled the frame,
Shaking lintel dust into the last red rays.
"The heather is from the original homestead;
it is the only thing pretty here.
The land has never weathered
and is harder than where we live;
it makes people old before their time.
I do not recognize anyone as family.
A storm came up on the crossing
and frightened me but brought us faster,
I pray for a storm to bring me home."
I went down to bed, grandmother brushed her long grey hair,
Grey and light like the lintel dust

Settling in the attic, settling on the heather,
The last buzzing flies. My eyes were heavy,
I could see the dust,
The rock was crumbling in the yard.

Family Drives

My brother and sister and I set fire
to the first family car I remember,
a 1940 Ford my grandfather bought
with some of the money he got
for the million board feet of timber
he cut out of his sugar bush
ruined by the hurricane of '38.
We were playing in it in the yard
and somehow the cigarette lighter
caught fire, or the wiring behind.
There were calls and swearing
and me looking through the dash
as through a keyhole of perdition's door.
My folks replaced the car with a 1951 Chevy,
five years out of date, and drove it
till coming home from a Christmas concert
a cold snowy night, poor tires and ice
combined to make us skip the ditch
and crack a tree. With dad pushing
and young children pretending, we got
in out onto the road and backed it down
the hill. That was the last time it went
backwards because it lost reverse
so we had to plan trips carefully.
Finally the one to the car dealer's
where my father parked the nose hard against
a wall and bought a 1952 almost the same
except grey instead of black.
Black would have been more appropriate
if we'd completed the trip we started
over the cliff into Hartwell Pond.
On an icy road a truck did not get over
and my family all stared straight down

at the black ice we would have plunged through,
like my father's brother's brand new car
coasting into the farm pond when he used it
to get cows one cold morning,
except a four inch maple held us.
The car lasted beyond that,
but winter hills were often beyond it,
tractionized tires not good,
the machine at the garage even puncturing one
my father wanted done and they put a liner
and new tube in it because he could afford
no other. My mother's younger brothers blew
their first car up one winter by pouring
gasoline into the carburetor
and though the car was cold blooded
cold mornings, they heated it
through and through. The youngest's face
took years to repair. Two summers later,
driving to the oldest brother's wedding,
changing places on the move, they rolled
their convertible onto guard rails.
The car was totalled; the only injury
was a permanent hole through one uncle's arm.
My youngest uncle rolled my grandfather's car
over three times in a field
and did the same to a garage loaner.
We thought that with the English Opel,
only two years old, we had it made.
Two months later we ran head on
into a neighbor's lumber laden truck
and it shortened the car, by half,
but luckily none of our lives
though I can still see my mother's
swollen face through which she could not.
All the family recalls the '55 Chevy

as a good car, though the engine
fell out three times and the last time,
coming home from church, the mounts
broke so badly it couldn't be repaired.
We passed it for a couple of weeks
in bright fall weather, the car blue
like the sky and my mother said
it would make a fine lawn ornament.
The '57 we got to replace it lasted
less than the winter. We had to house heifers
at a neighbor's barn and several freshened
so morning and night we took milking machines,
and when hay ran out there, bales,
and when the pipes froze, milk cans of water,
and ruined the back springs.
One night a late passerby came
to the door and told us the car was on fire.
The backseat was dragged out in flames.
For the next weeks, riding in front,
we could look back and watch the universal
joint turn its housing bright red.
My father's father, who had fled
when my father was ten, died
of a heart attack in his car that spring.
His black Pontiac had an amber face
of a chief on its hood that pleased us boys
but was no more hard set than my father's
as he drove that car hard through mud season
till he finally ripped the transmission out
bringing us home from sugaring one deep night.
A '57 Ford was next, the car
I learned to drive a car in.
I'd been driving tractors and trucks
since eight. My father's brother drove
truck from about the same age.

Early on he was driving a 1921 International
in haying and didn't know how
to start again on a hill. He coasted backwards
then flipped the truck and took
the cab off cleanly. They had to finish
so my grandfather straightened the steering column
and sat him on a kitchen chair on the frame.
He remembers the scratch of hay
on his neck and back. The truck I drove
the most, a long bed Ford farm truck,
was ruined when my father burned the brakes out
coming home with a load of slab wood
we'd loaded for sugaring. When we got
to my uncle's they threw water on
to douse the flames. We spent two hours
unloading cedar, drove the crawler on
and started for our place, but the differential
was ruined and wouldn't get us up
the first steep hill. My father yelled
and one by one us kids jumped for the snowbanks
from the back, and mother and the baby
from the cab. My father rode it till it struck
a bank above the bridge. The cab stood up nicely
and took a little bow and the crawler
slid and spun off the bed and drove its blade
about a foot into the ground. Father started
it, the lags tore the bed edge to kindling,
but he got it down; I drove it home.
It was that crawler with which he tried
to get us up a hill one sleety Sunday
but the crawler turned sideways
above the car and the lags were like ice skates,
he clocked a pretty good speed
right into the front end. My mother finished
the job on her way to school one winter day.

She took a corner wide and didn't kill herself
or the other driver when she hit her head on.
Earlier that year my mother's father had done
the same with my grandmother riding.
Her head went through the windshield,
her scalp was ripped back
and her entire face was as blue and swollen
as the grapes that grew on their back porch.
The next winter my youngest aunt was driving
her '55 Chevy convertible in late fall
over rutted roads and a rut threw
the car off into a tree that drove the engine
through the fire wall and broke her leg.
Her brothers had gotten her such an old car,
all they could afford, after my grandfather had
turned a tractor on its back onto him
and crushed himself slowly before he was found.
When they brought him home and laid him
on his couch it was as if he'd fallen
asleep after work, which is the way
I'd like to think of it but can't.
I thought of much of this when laid up
for a time when my own 40's car
that I had for college was struck
by a lumber truck running a stop sign
as I raced from class to work. In that car
I felt like the hero of an American movie,
an ordinary man a little unsure of all
that surrounds him but moving ahead,
a family left behind in the country, bucolic
pleasant lies the cinema told me.
Lying there I saw the sharp edges of things,
as if sitting in a drive-in on a crisp evening;
and years later returning from work at two
in the morning when I woke to a shatter of sparks

as though I was trying to arc weld the car
I was driving to the rails;
I saw patterns, a family driven.

Tree Climbing

I only knocked myself out once.
I was picking apples,
chose a too thin or badly attached branch
and drove my head straight down
and right back up between my shoulder blades
and seemed to lie with the dead
my mother said, who bent and breathed
into me. Not dead or not going to die
I finally rose and leaning
on my mother's and brother's shoulders
walked home, my spine feeling
like a snapped jag of old apple wood.
My father had broken his arm and shoulder
falling from a pine when young.
I had fallen, but not from the top,
of the eighty foot maple I climbed
to the top to long from.
I had fallen from birches I swung,
and pin cherries in the tree lines of fields,
landing on field stone,
and mountain ash and willows so supple,
and wild plums, the crushed fruit
in my hands and hair, and most kinds of apple trees,
and beech trees when trying to get the nuts
before the squirrels and chipmunks,
and oaks and ash and basswood,
and pines, whose bark was easy to carve,
and spruces, dense branches sticking and poking,
and firs, whose popped resin blisters stained the hands
and stung the eyes,
but I had never been more than scratched.
Now I lay on the couch two days
till I could move my neck.

I longed to be above the attending pain
and others' attendance,
I longed to sit in the soft wood saddle
of my favorite branches,
riding out the wind's buckings,
easily swallowing the dappled air.

My Brother on Fire

I remember the dance he did,
a reel, first alone,
then with my mother
as he whirled around the kitchen
with flames climbing the arm
and side of his sweater
towards his face, and he turning
his face and pulling his head
as if he were trying to get away
from himself and my mother,
who had turned to him already
afire from reaching across the stove
for some newly made sweet.
She finally held him close
to her to smother the fire
in the folds of her robe.
They stood there on the day
of the winter solstice,
having completed their firedance,
much as my ancestors
on the year's darkest day
might have stood having danced
around a smoldering peat fire,
the smell of once living matter burning
filling the room or rooms,
and in my family's house too
at least the promise and celebration
of long days to come.

Summer Dusk

In our Studebaker eight
With mother at the wheel
We arrive at the house on High Street
And creep through the halls
Quiet as thieves,
Afraid of the crones and haggard men
Who stand in the doors
Or peer from cribs of steel.
My father's great aunt waits on the highest floor,
The floor below the widow walk she walks
Though never a widow.
We find her by the window
Humming to herself.
She extends her bitten hands.
I've always grown so much for her
And yet she's never satisfied.
Why does she care?
How close, after all, is a great great aunt?
Farther than a grandmother,
Closer than a fly.
Her room is the color of old varnish.
"It's so depressing.
I ache to get fresh air
And my flowers can get no sun."
She gave my sister a cactus
That sprouted new ones for years,
Flowing from pot to pot
Till mother threw them out.

It gets late.
At our leaving she pouts,
Tongue always pushing her lower lip,
Old pet.

The lawn is suffused in the blue-green light
Of afterdusk that she wishes for her room.
Toads are feeding in the dew;
Leaving I almost step on them,
Pop eyes scanning the horizon,
And when flies' flights coincide
The whip tongues strike,
The brown huddled bodies barely move.
They do not peep now,
It is not the time of year to sing.

I turn in the backseat. She is standing in the window,
Her blotched face and hands seem white.
I'm safe enough in my retreat to wave goodbye
And mean it, a fierce civility.

Turkey Sticking

The school room was small,
the only room but for a cloak room
and an adjoining hallway to the two-holer.
The owner had spent his whole school youth
toward the front in order to see
the blackboard, now used for chalking
up numbers of turkeys slain.
The fine hardwood floor was covered
in turkey manure, feathers, blood.
The windows frosted more than ever
as neighbors helped him
in a late fall loose change earning chore.
Bent wires hung from old light fixtures.
Turkeys were snagged,
legs looped with baling twine,
were dangled down for the one person stuck
with thrusting the knife
through the roof of the mouth into each brain,
no jerking contractions, tight muscles,
misses of the chopper's block.
Wings were clipped for dusters
for the women and for sale,
the softest feathers saved for down,
the rest rained on we who looked up,
grown-ups sitting for a moment,
children who'd taken a break from cold games.
When small, I was once lifted by an adult
onto a new pine table and put in a turkey bag
of white down where I was not found
for three rounds of hide-and-seek.
I suffered a child's fear of suffocation,
light breaths. I smelled pine,
and the tar on people's hands,

manure and urine, iron, iron of blood,
the copper taste of fear, the fire and smoke
of the last pin feathers being singed,
the singed skin of the bodies piled around me.
Against exposed skin I felt feathers
as light as my own eyelashes,
their white was blindingly dark.
I could hear soft talk, as if foreign,
from a land I did not yet know,
worried talk, and children's anxious questions,
my homeland. I had vanished.
For one of the few times in my life
I knew then and know now
I was joyful to be sought not seeking.

Public Health

My father laid on the principal's desk
and had his tonsils taken out.
They went through the school in a day,
during the war, when they were trying to save
health, and time, and beds.
Father laid on the gym floor for an hour
with the others, then went home.

Years later my sister and brother and I stood
in front of a door at the town hall,
a line of children wending through,
screams on the other side, tears on this side.
We did not know after this
we would not spend our lives in an iron lung,
would not become cripples as a favorite cousin had.
My sister bent close.
Mother had cut her long blonde hair
for first grade, she looked like a lovely boy.
"They are going to take your tonsils out,
and probably other things. The shot
may give you polio. Don't cry."
The last injunction assuring I would,
no promise they were done after one painful prick
could stop me. The grown ups had
little sympathy, had seen enough
to know fear's full dose,
were trying to act wisely
in the face of possible and known
failure and folly.

A Few Deaths in the Family

My father's mother died of breast cancer
in her mid fifties, it was hard,
as it was when my mother's father,
in his early sixties, crushed
himself with a tractor,
but it could be said they lived good lives,
as was said for great uncles, aunts.
Children's deaths tore.
Some could go by almost unnoticed,
my mother's oldest brother's wife's stillborn one,
and late miscarriage the next year,
my uncle and aunt the only two graveside
with the minister, but at car doors,
front doors the family performed
its small ceremonies of talk and blessing.
At the death of the second uncle's baby
a few weeks old, the wrenching could be heard.
I heard it when my brother, one month old,
died after an operation to let him eat.
My mother had spent the summer hoping
for a girl, he was born in fall and died in fall.
The hospital had called my grandparents
to bring my parents to be with him
as they had called four years before
to have them there as I died of whooping cough.
I did not die, my brother did.
I saw my father crying the next morning
as he did the chores a farmer must,
my mother wept between the house and barn
and sat us on the porch and said
perhaps God was punishing her
for wanting a girl too hard.
Few tears of grief and none of regret

were shed when a first cousin
who'd married her first cousin
lost her second born. The oldest, a girl,
saw her father carry the six-toed sibling,
boy or girl no one asked or was told,
down to the furnace to burn their shame,
and she was haunted by it for years,
her parents would not talk.
Their fourth born lived five years
but never crawled, or walked, or talked.
I remember him at junior missionary meetings,
who were we to save, where he would lie
by the door jamb like a stop,
then his life did.
Mother's first cousin's girl
was my age. In her last remission
we sat on the hay in the full barn
by the upper windows on a sunny day.
The light streaming through
shone right through her ears
as if they were almost clear wax.
We had kissed there the year before,
we did not kiss that day,
I held her hand, so mad
I wanted her to die that minute.
Two cousins, one adopted, first cousins
to each other, got cancer, a rare form,
from some agent on their farms.
At church, at meetings, we all watched
their progress down.
The native born survived somehow,
the adopted not, to die at home in exile.
My second uncle lost an adopted girl
when she tried to jump the auger
emptying silage to the cows.

It caught her clothes and tore and sliced
her unto death.
Mother's fourth brother's boy died at five
when I was twelve. I had helped care
for him one vacation, he would sit
with me at church and I would dandle
him and he called me daddy.
His uncle held him one day haying
and he said he hurt but they kept on.
My two uncles took him to the hospital
next day, he said he could sit up for them,
but two days later, soon after he had said,
in one of those statements that is a child's question,
he would be fine, the delirium of meningitis
took him, and took him.
My own son is five now.
I do not worry about his death
but he said recently he does not want
many numbers in his age
because he does not want to die,
and he said if he is at the dying place
he will get in the truck and drive home
and will take me too,
and I am reminded that he was born
on my dead brother's birthday
at the same time.
How much more we are than what we seem,
bearing mankind's knowledge and longing,
and how much less, the whole body ready
to work and live except for some
large or small part that cannot.
On the day my five year old cousin died
my father and I were trying to start
the crawler, working on the motor.
When mother told us, he just said   No

and chained the too light tractor
to the heavy crawler to pull me
along to try and jump start it.
I see that whole damn green field through tears,
my father driving ahead, blurred, raving angry,
the lags rattle along then skid
each time I pop the clutch at speed,
the cold engine not wanting to turn or fire.
Each time I do that the front
of his tractor rises as if to overturn
but he cranks his engine up again,
we weave and careen, he yelling,
me sobbing, sobbing for my cousin,
and out of the terror
    at each release of the clutch
that I will be the weight that kills him.

Riding in the Open

Spring, summer, and into fall
we children rode in the open
on wagons, trailers, the backs
of flat-bed trucks, and pick-ups.
All of them, loaded or unloaded,
moving faster than they should.
In spring we rode sap loads,
holding on with hands no glove
or mitten could keep warm in the wet,
and sloshing sap filling our boots,
mud and stones thrown by the wheels
marking our clothes and faces.
In summer we often rode the loads of hay.
Our work was pressed, by the amount
still in the field, or rain, or darkness.
If the load were not placed right,
off it would go over a bump
or up a hill or around a corner,
bales splayed out over bends, bushes,
ditches, and some of us
scrambling out unscathed or scathed.
My sister was swiped off the highest load
ever put on the truck
by a then too low branch,
the breath knocked out of her
but not for good.
Once a new hired man drove
the wagon off the road
when meeting a truck
as I dangled my legs over
the off road side.
The snap of maple whips carried
me off and under and I could have kissed

the wheel as it passed my head
but only my foot was ground
into the dirt by the tread.
My uncle was hard put
to decide whether to hold me
or the man's neck
and chose me.
Coming out of a steep field
with the long bed truck piled high
the whole back end of the load
caved off and three of us rode
the fall to the hard ground.
Someone was always racing to town
for more twine or for parts
to machinery busted by hard use
and old age. We young would hold on
to the back of the pick-up cab,
our hair straight back,
tears of speed in our eyes,
or stand on twenty or thirty-
five gallon cans of gasoline
tied on the flat-bed's back.
We would reach up to catch leaves,
fumes in our lungs,
try to keep our balance
over the rough roads,
hold onto each other's legs
as we stretched out over the side
to grab grasses and flowers in passing.
It all ended each year in fall with cold coming,
but not before we rode
loads of chopped corn home,
the green damp in our boots
and clothes and lungs
as we sped from the fields

to pitch and kick the corn
into the blower's auger and tried not to fall
into that invention, which took
lives each year.
We survived all those years
like most of the farm children we knew.
When I speak of those rides
I think of how we mostly could not talk,
mouths agape,
cheeks puffed out by the force of wind,
any conversation blown back passed us,
ears wind stopped,
and of the holding on,
and in the face of the black despair
we were all prone to,
wild laughter.

Sledding

The longest run was a mile and a half,
starting from a neighbor's yard,
down his quarter mile drive
onto the main road.
We mostly slid at night to tell
if cars were coming,
no stopping at the corner
except by ditching at forty miles an hour,
blood and fractures either way.
A flat section was next,
then the steep falling off
and long run past home.
We rattled over ruts,
tried to hold a steady line.
Fastest down the final pitch,
fifty and better, teeth rattling
from the iron runners, cold, fear.
The coast out at the end was shortened
by foot dragging to shorten
the long haul back,
ropes caught in the cold crooks of our hands,
the trudge taking long enough
so that three or four runs a night
were all we could manage.
Sometimes the road was so icy
we could not walk it
but strode in the banks.
Those nights the slightest mis-steer
sent the back set of runners on the travis
fish-tailing out of control,
the five or six riders trying
not to hit the banks or trees
or tip off and be run over

by the metal that sparked
on road grit like the 4th of July.
The riders thought of past
twisted ankles and broken legs
and opened heads, and those accidents
kept our foolishness
to the foolishness of the ride itself,
a roller coaster fear, a bobsled fear,
knowing the sled could skip
the tracks and banks at any time
and play you out over the wide white landscape.

He Who Was Missing His Pals

They, who had slid in winter
down hills that had small cliffs
they sailed over and dropped
ten or twenty feet and ran
the way out to the road
on the bent sheets of roofing steel
that could have sawed them to the bone;
who had walked with skill
the barn bay beams
and had fallen to floors
they could recover from
not the full five floors to stone;
who had raced workhorses bareback
in pastures of glacial till
and worried not about rocks but cow shit;
who built, as the barns were filled,
caves under the tons of hay
through which they could push and squeeze
the narrow way back
toward the heat of summer;
who had become lost to him;
who now drove trucks   raised grain,
poured concrete   raised steel;
who were simply separated in ways
and at distances beyond understanding;
they were often in his dreams,
often dying beyond his saving.
He had not had to mourn them in his youth,
now mourned their passing from him
while they all lived
with darkness, light, heat, speed.

Bullies

This one squeezed my friend's neck
till a blood vessel broke in his head
he went to reform school
did not finish school
was shipped home from Vietnam dead

Another one stole from our lunch pails
no matter what we did or said
now lives by the market
owns his own slaughterhouse
and keeps himself very well fed

This one flung firewood at us
he stood by the pile, we fled
later he burned down his home
clapped on the lawn
as his family watched the sky turn red

An older boy raped a classmate
under spruce trees, where she bled
he never was punished
a few of us knew
saw a little of the terror ahead

This one scarred brothers and sisters
in fields, in the barn, the shed
hopes for forgiveness
but expects none
lives a full lonely life instead

Breakwater

He and I stand on the breakwater
After walking the huge blocks of this digit
Just to stand. He looks back,
But mostly looks out to sea and says,
"This is long, but not as long
As the one at the beach on Normandy."
I say I hadn't known they put up breakwaters
To land. "Hell no, not to land.
When they shipped me back —us back —
They had me in a cast up to my chest,
A bar between my legs. They bundled me about
Like a Jesus suitcase, wheeled me down
Their made-up pier on a baggage cart;
I saw the new made port then."
I seldom heard him talk of the war,
Never heard him swear. His hair,
The color of granite, turned
When he was seventeen. "They have a causeway
Over there they call the Giant's Causeway."
"I thought in Scotland," I interrupt.
"Yes, well, it was on the way,
And all the same from here. Christ,
We felt like giants when the convoy made it,
But we'd shrunk back to size by the time
We reached the line."
His daughter, my wife, and her mother
Stand on a thin line of beach.
Beside the rocks they too are small.
"I don't know why they don't come out."
"It's not something they do," I say,
Then I see them pointing, pointing and waving,
I cannot see at what
Then what looks like a buoy.

44

"Seal," he says, "saw thousands of them
On the off islands, coming back on a Polish ship
That had sailed from the Germans at the start
And wound up carrying racks of wrecked men—
Spent all that money converting her
To a hospital ship and still so uncomfortable—
And Jimmy, bunk above me, worried about wolf packs, says,
'I'd like to be a seal, they'd never see me
Slip away instead of slipping under like I'll do
Dressed up in all this plaster.'
'You'd get eaten no matter what,' I told him."
This story as fragmented as his leg had been,
As the bridge his battalion had won,
As every man of his company but two,
As the rocks beneath our feet
As big as boxcars, with the faint illusion of movement.
"Let's go back," he says.
I know he means it simply,
But I stand looking at a sea
That means more than what it is,
Having heard him talk of death and fear,
And behind it and us something as close as love.
For a moment, I'd rather not go in any direction.

Deconstruction

The forty foot hand hewn beam fell,
hit one end on the stone foundation
and snapped in half, even from our height
we could smell the smell
of one hundred and fifty year old dry wood.
We laughed. The last floor
of the huge barn coming down.
We'd started months before
by ripping thousands of cedar shingles
from the roofing boards with catspaws
and long claw hammers.
We untied the windbeams
then loosened the thirty foot rafters
and sent them singing off the queen post
horizontal and top sill
from which smoke rose as each length
singed the wood as it sped over
before sailing free
and each one's end imbedding
itself feet in the surrounding soil.
We stripped the sheathing, two-story long
pine boards in a double layer,
cut nails making a solid line across
the top of each. We saved the good nails
in a found pail, not saving the boards
for the sake of expediency.
Then the beams. The long work
pounding out the trunnels
with round iron bars and small sledges
bent by bent, working each floor down,
queen post, major girt, wall, high drive,
middle girt, sill, and joists for all.
Sometimes we dismantled beam by beam,

in places we pulled whole sections down
with block and tackle or comealong.
Once I stood in the middle
as four beams landed around me,
the look on my sister's face
as though she were about to cradle
me in death, but no injury there
and surprisingly few all through.
One huge bruise on my upper thigh
where a beam snapped and kicked back
and its end drove hard, and a welt
on the back of my head when my brother-in-law
eased the tension on a holding rope
and a quarter brace fell
on my bent over frame
and buckled me a while.
The anti-racking summer beam
was near the last, we lifted
its tenon out of its dove-tail mortise
in the forty footer.
We felled the last small host of uprights,
then everything was down
to the sill which sat
on its mortarless foundation
as straight as the day it was laid,
but dirt lay high around it
so rot had invaded and we let it lay.
The good beams we loaded on wagons
and carted to a house site.
Also, trunnels, cut nails, a few granite slabs,
the silo liner boards, worn smooth
and stained by years of ensilage.
The rest we burned on a rainy day,
kerosene and careful stacking of part
to get it raging, then the whole scene clear.

With the knowledge we've gleaned
from the taking down,
things to do and not to do,
we hope we're ready to start anew,
left with our stacked and numbered pieces,
left with our own devices.

Terrane of the Bed

The small country changes
every few minutes.
The spread becomes the velt
and a lion or cheetah roars
his roar in our ears
and our two year old weaves
stealthily toward our heads;
or the sheets are shoals
the sailor only manages to evade
and sometimes washes up on one
and two lighthouses flash
from the headlands;
or he is a man or goat climbing
mountains as they're forced up,
leaping crevasses as they form.

His parents are like demiurges,
having some small say and power of suggestion
over this small province and its inhabitant
who will achieve the world soon enough
but for now settles on this terrane
floating where he wills.

Averruncation

Late fall chores
that can be done no earlier:
pruning — my own trees and a friend's —
the sugars stored safely in roots
for next year's growth,
the air so cold sap no longer runs
so the cuts stay dry and clean,
hand pruners for spurs, twigs, water shoots,
pole shears for large branches
or those too high, I sometimes must appear
a circus balancing act, long pole guided
among the uprights and horizontal structures
of these fruiting spaces,
moving quickly as targets fall;
mulching — I think of the circus again,
more hay for the animals — rose bushes,
raspberries, strawberry beds, flowers,
so that the expansion and contraction
of the earth in thaw and freeze
won't shear the roots, a more likely death
than from the cold itself.

My friend lives in a large city
to the south. I live where I was born,
where he has bought a summer home.
My life here has a side to it that depends
on resourcefulness that his does not.
His requires a certain vigilance.
There is satisfaction in this spectrum,
but sometimes he wishes to settle more,
give up the cross country shuttle,
be more solidly founded,
and I would like to trim my roots,
to take this impossible show on the road.

Lave

I took friends
to the site of an old mill.
The whole building had been bolted
to a slanting rock the stream fell
across in one long slide.
Stream and rock and bolts remained.
Hot day. We held our children
in the stream. Dry moss on the rock
was slick and green under water.
One friend and his little girl
got too close, they made no cries
but arms flailed the dazzle green air,
and a terrible humor rose as we watched them
bump and spray down the rocky chute.
Lunging for them I thought of my uncle
sliding down the hay chute
and opening his neck on a bolt.
When they landed in the bottom pool
our terror turned to excitement
as they stood up safely, clean.

Corn Roasts

Tassles top the corn rows
that line the road, corn silk
dangles, still gold, drying
to black later when raccoons, bears,
and thunderstorms will have brought
whole patches of stalks down.
More often in my youth than now
farmers would plant two or three rows
of sweet corn woodside as an earlier
ripening attraction to keep
the depredation low.
One old woman I knew would have a corn roast
every fall from the bounty found
in those long rows, baskets and baskets
of bright yellow corn gone to starch
brought in by hired hands.

Sparks would leap and flare and settle.
The bonfire would attract those who knew
and the curious just driving by.
All would park down low among the ledges
and walk up through cow pies, thistle,
in the almost dark to where the lit brush
and wood and busted furniture stood
piled higher than any human,
and through all the years she had them,
flaring higher then any second growth tree
in the surrounding woods.

The woman who held the roasts
also acted Shakespeare every summer
with her volunteer troupe.
She, in lead roles, exhorted

soldiers, rebels, exiles;
we stood as pikemen, archers, hangers-on.
She also ran a private library
visited almost every week by everyone
in the church. Farmers and their wives
borrowed biographies, novels, histories
of the dark ages and numberless wars;
and their children children's books
whose pages turned easily, turned, become other.

We would all stand shoulder to shoulder
holding long sticks like pikestaves
surmounted with corn cobs
lowered to and raised from the fire.
We were like crusaders or Romans the night
before battle, or the night
after, holding aloft
heads of those conquered. All we needed
was to find an errant boar
for the picture and action to be complete.
The light on our faces
showed a peaceful mob,
and here and there an asbestos-gloved man
would be hauling unhusked corn
from the ashes where it had been tossed.

A friend of mine tells me roasting corn
reminds him of braziers in the streets of Cairo
in his youth, when corn grown in the delta
was a treat. I wonder with him
when that crop found its way there.
He had never known steamed corn,
just swollen starchy kernels bursting
in their husked seams.
I knew it so on a green but charring hillside

as unknowingly all those gathered helped reenact
the bivouacs of armies my ancestors might have been,
that my friend's ancestors might have seen,
uneasy on unfamiliar ground,
with the pleased and nervous faces
of people who have partaken
of crops not their own.

After the Time Change

My little boy is eating currants
frost dried but still juicy,
fingers prodding among leafless twigs.
These will be the last,
he has eaten them for months.
A few raisin-like near-rotten grapes
are his next target, he laughs to himself.
I am pruning an elderly neighbor's raspberries,
my gloves not quite thick enough,
the ground not quite dry enough,
but the day mild though windy
and his conversation bracing.
He tells of a bobcat hunt.
He and a friend set their dogs free
early of a January evening
and sat by the swamp drinking coffee
till they heard the dogs take trail
and begin to move away, beyond where baying
would carry back. The two were already
in but falling behind. They both ran them
till ten the next morning.
His friend said give up but my neighbor knew
the dogs would kill themselves running
or stay by the treed cat till they all
succumbed and though he thought he might
he pushed on having moved miles past
where he knew he was. Close to midnight
he could hear the dogs again though weakly
and they weak when he got to the tree.
Got them and the cat
and still had a two hour walk to the road
for his trouble, but his friend
was there, having figured the likeliest

route that they all would take.
When he got too old for such exploits
he hunted the hills behind our places
or just ran his dogs, rabbit dogs then.
It got so he never took his gun,
knew the rabbits almost by name,
but late one season some fellows,
as he called them, went ahead
and killed the rabbits and hung them
from the trees. The gun he carried
will be my boy's. He remembers when he was
ten, riding down to town one day
his father said they'd better run on
to the store and get a rifle.
He wants my boy to remember him by it
though I hope he will live for that
to be the least of it. My boy already slides
on a sled the man's father got him
the same year as the rifle.
Lost once in Stillwater Swamp he laid
the rifle in the direction
he thought he should go and climbed
a tree to check and adjust.
My boy and I go to his house often
and each time look at owls he has
in his study: long-eared, great-horned,
barred, and saw-whet, plus an osprey, and deer;
and a picture of his father sitting before
most of the owls that he himself shot.

My neighbor tries to bend and lift
too big a bunch of brambles,
"I'm like a rusty old car
with pieces falling off in the road."
With his car, that will no longer pass inspection,

he's gotten mountains of leaves
from all over town, stacked them for mulch
covered with pine needles to keep them in place.
"Didn't know to do that and one year
on a day like this I watched them all
heading for the river. I just
sort of saluted them with the rake as they went."
My boy is on his back watching leaves
from the willow tree rain by.
He asks if there are any raspberries
and my neighbor says not for a long time,
next year. We all walk slowly back
toward his porch where birds are eating
at a feeder. They don't really belong there,
or here at all this time of year,
confused voices in a squabble for order.
He holds the railing to take the steps.
"My rope's running out and I forgot
to tie a knot in the end."
My boy races for home, laughs,
and I do too despite the pain of my hands,
red worn spots and blisters, like rope burns.

Winter Stay in a Peat Bog

Cold runs downhill
and in this great bowl
collects like a physical thing.
At 40 below zero
I can hear the air sizzle
as moisture turns to ice,
and now and then a tree will ring
like a bell as it splits
its length. I can believe
I'm gaining knowledge
of how a friend in northern Labrador lives,
and when I fall on my skis
and tumble down a pitch,
I think of him falling down a slope
with too great a load of caribou
frozen to the shape of his back
but unyieldingly heavy,
how hard it was to rise.
I'm camping here several days,
could die I suppose,
but not brave
or in much danger, just cold.
At night I listen to coyotes bark
on the trail. I'm glad I'm sleeping,
but I walk the trail each night
as Orion swings his sword
between the walls of trees.
Waking in deep woods in deep winter
is like rising in mid-spring at home,
a thin but solid wall of bird song.
The birds gather where I urinate,
they eat the mineral stained snow.
One day I found tracks across fresh snow,

feet and tail tracks as if all in a flurry,
but all on the surface
like some Jesus lizard of snow had passed
and crossed the bog
where even now the rot below
sends mist up through snow vents.
Then I see rags of birch bark,
loose pages of the world's manuscript,
that the wind has stripped from the trees
and walked through the snow,
how light and soon passing their passage.
Behind me
is my whole trail to this point.

How Birds Fly

Another poem of hospital rooms, a genre all their own.
I would say this room did not contain you,
held only the artifact of your body,
but you were there.
The first days were long, lurid,
how each lump increased or moved,
which muscles failed in which maneuver,
what bodily functions ceased or started
with no guidance from you.
But as the numbers of tubes and fluids
increased, we had wondrous talks.
You asked about the woman climbing
up the hospital walls, carefully placing
her ladder and leading her children,
the youngest with dark large glasses,
up to where they could see you clearly.
You told of the dog walking around you,
keeping at bay too numerous visitors,
his tail long and curled, like his lip
except when he licked your hand.
A man sometimes stood to the right
of your headboard, white dinner jacket,
red handkerchief. He reminded you
of Xavier Cugat, movies of your childhood
in the local town hall, dance halls
where your mother danced with strange men;
often he would bend and tap your shoulder.

The woman you lived with carved birds
and she and I talked of those we spotted
en route. You asked why you felt
like you were inside a great black bird
driving it like a bus. I was grateful

and sad you did not know.
For the last five days of your life
you took yourself off medication,
had yourself taken home,
no more wonder. The days not long,
eating like a bird,
fragile as a bird,
driving the black bird hard.

Over the Edge

He is set to rappel into the old quarry.
The rope loops a yellow birch
that over arches the granite face.
He is in shadow but the birch's yellow leaves
shine above him in the fall air.
The water below is a pure navy blue,
an effect of light and the admixture
of carbonate minerals leeching out
of the slate and granite
and the tannin of all the leaves
that have fallen and drifted in.
He thinks of the thick layers
of leaves, of the millions of leaves
off just one tree multiplied
and falling, almost no weight.
On land, the leaves become soil,
rotting to a fine humus,
but in this cold water the strata,
individual leaves, were probably recognizable
years' worth of layers down.
He had dived in summer from almost as high,
but stepped out here horizontal,
his back to the water
belly to the sky, descending,
his feet finding the star drill marks.
He thinks of the woman he loves,
of her yellow red hair spread above him.
He thinks of blackness,
and of things lasting for years,
but not of falling,
only of being supported, held.

Ferris Wheel Out My Window

A six pointed star whirls in the center,
the image is centered in my window
at some distance on the edge of town.
It happens that in that direction
when the fair's not here
there is only darkness at night.
The carnival unfolds each year,
takes over that quadrant of sky.
As a boy I knew dark skies year round,
could only just make out that light
over a distant hill, only went twice
at night then. The once I went
with my grandfather we rode the ferris wheel
five times. He had ridden the first ones
to come here only a decade or two
after their first invention.
My son and I ride many times,
feel gravity loosen its grip
for a moment at the top,
and feel its hold tighten
at the moment of lifting.
How light and solid we feel,
he feels, beside me under my hand.
A woman friend took her daughter,
both of them afraid of heights,
but they rode away from the earth for fun.
When they walked back to this house
their faces showed how much better
it had been for what they had overcome.
The girl lay at the foot of her bed
that night to fall asleep and wake
to dreams made real out her window.
With fainter light out this window

above us all the oldest side show,
the great wheel of the Milky Way
spinning through the gim-crackery continuum.
My son and I sit again for a short time
in our short ride
on its long run.

Driving by Moonlight

I began as a teenager to drive
long distances, empty highways
and back roads, in bright moonlight
without using headlights,
turning the dash lights off
the better to see. In summer
the moon had to be full or almost
for enough light to filter through
the darkest tunnels of trees.
Cows faces loomed beyond or over fences,
huge eyes, like seeing an octopus
in the murky deeps. Shadows themselves
sometimes appeared physical.
Billboards advertised only the darkness
that contained them.
Speed was hard to figure,
lacking most visual clues,
but with the window rolled down
I could hear my rush
in the grasses and bushes I passed.
In winter a full moon would light
that snow covered world brighter
than the sun would an overcast day,
the albedo of that northern land so high
I could watch owls hunting the roads I drove.
The roads were an easy hunting grounds
small animals continually crossed
or travelled along, I would often see
their tracks or movement.
On certain cold clear winter nights
I did not even need the moon,
the light of the stars was enough.
The stars themselves seemed to flow

over the car like snow caught in the draft.
I drive this way still sometimes, always alone.
After a while, with night vision, averted vision,
I see more clearly dimmer magnitudes.

On the Longe

The stud circles warily
his first day on the longe
since breeding season.
He has covered eighteen mares
and thinks there may be more,
but human use is his function now.
The training circle is packed
and his hooves clop as on pavement.
I do not worry about head set
this day because he is watching
every pasture, every lane.
The lanes are empty, the brood mares move
in unison over timothy and red top.
I'm not used to this either and get dizzy.
I let him all the way out to slow
him down, bring him to a walk and set
for canter. As he moves off, too fast,
I wonder who first thought of taming
horses for any use whatsoever,
but am glad I do not have to create
a pattern but follow rules developed
over generations by many others, and my family,
until here I stand, firmly holding on,
turning. At the circus once, I watched
the equestrian acrobats keep shortening
the check reins until the horses' chins
were against their necks
because there was a storm and the canvas
flapped in the wind and rapped
like a drum in the driving rain
and made the horses nervous
and very high stepping
so they were beautiful to watch,

67

with necks curved and feet flying,
and almost impossible to control.

With work in both directions done
my horse and I walk off, pass by apple trees
for a treat for both of us.
My back aches, his will.
We will stand off several days running,
working him into pulling evenly and long,
leaning into the collar at my command
and moving such a load of timber
as I could only imagine water moving,
his muscles that liquid and smooth.
I unsnap the chain and caveson, and set
him free, trot, road trot, walk, canter.

II

Milk Run

I stayed in the Balcones Highlands,
those limestone tiers of Texas
on which no water sits
but drains to cracks and caverns,
and in that dry heat drank
more milk than usual.
It took two runs a week, thirty miles
each way, try for more milk
and it would spoil. She and I
would crank up the air conditioning
and I would drive down off those hills
at better than a hundred heading
towards the Rio Grande,
passing on the way a Hollywood
reconstruction of the Alamo
now a remote desert tourist spot
to which we'd see a car or two straggling,
I'd toot, she'd wave, they'd stare.
The town was small, the grocery was,
the owner young but seasoned.
The first time I piled eight gallons
of milk on her counter
She said "Thirsty," then she asked
if I was paying with cash or check.
Said she preferred cash,
only the week before a handsome man
had come in and bought supplies
and paid with a check that was no good.
If she saw him again she said
she was going to take something back,
was going to start at his shoulder
and take a swatch of skin down across
his middle long and wide enough for a belt,

or maybe she'd take enough for a whole damn saddle.
I paid my cash.
The next time I added two cans of sardines
to my order. She asked are you going
to eat that or is that wolf bait.
Said her husband had bought fifteen
cases of sardines for wolf bait
and had put them out in her back room
and left before he'd used more than a few cans.
Said now she couldn't stand to eat the stuff
and couldn't sell much either.
Said she hoped she hadn't put me off it.
I had nothing to say.
Next time she asked if I had been
to any dances hereabouts.
I said it hadn't crossed my mind.
She said I ought to get my mind to working,
or something anyway, looked like
most of me worked fine.
I don't believe anyone has ever set
a trap for me, but I could see
a certain yawning in the distance.
The woman I was with was almost on her knees.
This was neither low comedy or high drama,
but I could feel my toes being stepped on,
the cinch tightening.

Drawn In

She and I drove and walked to the top
of the plateau. We could see
far out over the small gorge
and farther rangeland. Near at hand
was a ravine topped like an arbor
with mescalbean trees and Lacey's oaks.
It might lead back to the river,
to a lookout point, to a grassy opening,
to a cave, and we could not resist entering.
I picked up mescal pods.
"One seed could kill you," she said,
"but the indians used to make a drug."
We noted the fine tracery of the rare oaks
against a sky turning grey.
We saw the clouds loose walls of rain,
inverted skyscrapers of rain
I hoped would reach us
so we might remain under the new found outcrop.
Someone had drawn figures on the rock,
men and women standing and reclining,
birds on the wing, perhaps green kingfishers,
certainly scissor tailed flycatchers,
whose descendants circled now.
The rain did not reach us
not even the points, all virga.
We went out and stood under
huge loops and arches of rainrise.
We thought to return later,
copy the drawings, bring others.
We did none of these,
but the same human habits,
reactions and pleasure to first surprises,
that kept us from returning,
drew us in.

Fire Starter

When the man got out to the ranch buildings
from the interior, he said the fire
was small. We loaded drums
of water from the river, shovels,
blankets to wet, and headed back
across dry uplands, deep arroyos,
trough cattle traps, goat fencing,
the many miles to where the man,
who had no good explanation how it started,
said the fire was smoldering.
Mid-afternoon, she and I and he arrived
at the place he'd left mid-morning.
The fire had burned two miles downwind,
almost as wide, was popping
mesquite trees like roman candles,
and his buildings could be erased
from any maps they'd made it on to.
We stood and watched dumbfounded,
waited for the distant fire department
we'd called before we'd left, heard them coming,
playing their sirens now and again
along rutted ranch roads. The first one
missed the little side road we'd gone down,
jammed his brakes, the second
cracked him good. First driver got out
to look and swear and wave
the other back. They both came roaring down.
Driver got out again, looked at our drums
and laughed, walked closer to the fire
till a line of trees exploded
and he retreated to beside his pumper,
said to no one and the wide spaces,
"Shhit, all the water in the world

74

in't gonna put that out,"
and climbed aboard for home,
and I thought, of all the water
in the world, none of it's been here.
I think the rancher was tempted
to take his rifle from his back window
and shoot the fire starter,
but he looked to a distant horizon
where he said a canyon was
and said, "Just have to wait
for it to gully out."
The ten more days I stayed at the ranch
black smoke carried east
in back of hills, toward an unseen canyon.
She and I swam in the river after work,
smelled what smelled like the earth burning,
laughed at the stories,
failed when trying to shape our laughter
to face the fear of everything that matters.
That night had been the first night we made love,
soaking the blankets we lay on
so they were like those which we
were going to fight a long, wide fire.

The Woman Who Kept the Indian Baby's Ear

She found the baby in a cave
on her ranch.
The Indian child's body was desiccated,
perhaps born and dead in her long lifetime,
or there for hundreds of years.
The difference between her skin
and the baby's skin was not great.
She told me she held it
a long time when she found it.
She took the body home.
She had that old desire
to make art, and disassembled the small frame,
began to use the bones in collages,
two finger joints became earrings,
the skin was a vellum
for which she had no text or painting.
Authorities got wind of what she was doing,
the phrase she used,
made her wrap the entire body
in a parcel and put it back,
promise to never do such a thing again.
"Well I never," she said
as rage, and excuse, and apology.
She showed me the ear she kept
in a small box, stuffed with batting.
The ear's shape and color reminded me
of the loaves of bread shaped like ears
buried with mummies in Egypt
to help the gods hear prayers,
such few and quiet prayers
as the dead might raise.
I had no prayers for the child,
was put off, but not shocked, by her actions.

My reactions seemed to fit the time,
but in my still wish that this
now wholly mineral thing be made whole
I was made archaic,
made to hear the nothing it hears.

River Baths

After the day's nails
had been driven,
the sheet rock taped and floated,
a particular room's floor sanded
and stained, or, next day, varnished,
there was time for the river.
She and I would lay in that swath
of sun lit water
in a county where there was no other
except in winter flash floods
or summer thunderstorms, the highlands
like the roof of Texas
from which all water ran.
A little percolated down
to where very deep wells reached
and windmills turned and pumped
constantly, the working clank and gurgle
of old machinery never an annoyance.
We could hear the neighbor's running,
the gather of goats and cattle.
We would lay in the day's same suspension
and for the first time be cool.
We did not have to worry
about ticks or fire ants or chiggers
or scorpions in paint stripper
and between joists and in crawl spaces.
We were between sky and earth,
and though the surface V's of snakes
would sometimes urge us onto rocks,
we often floated till the stars came out,
the Water Carrier, Pisces,
Delphinus breaching the sky,
and it was hard to tell

which was air, which was water.
I would move toward the constellations
of her parts
about which the blackness cooled and warmed.

Sumac

Brindle sumac and brindle cows,
a jigsaw with white sky.
He and she rode around to find
material for her paintings.
"Soo-mac," she said.
"Shu-mac," he said, "s-u like in sugar."
"If I could take a medicine against you,
I would," she said. Both married.

Later he kissed her belly and her breasts
but she said no more and she said
if she could stand that
she could stand anything.
He kissed her just inside her left breast
and said, "Yes, well, there's a placebo
for your heart, which I'm bound to break."
"A sugar pill like acid."
He felt like an alchemist
who has suddenly, without trying,
turned the few grams of gold
he has amassed to lead.

Later still she sent a slide
of a painting. Here were splotches of red,
like blood, white like skin,
here was the puzzle:
of all the tastes their tongues would touch,
learning what's bitter, what's sweet,
who to tell.

White Lawn Chairs

The man and woman sat in two wooden lawn chairs
on a fall abandoned dock.
The had walked around the end of a fence
in water to sit, water to make
the ankles ache.

The oak ridge across the lake
was thoroughly rusted and crumbling.
Three small boats on a long weathered dock
were the last bright color.
She was cold.

They had simply arrived here
without knowing the lake or camp were here.
When she asked if they were lost
he used the old saying,
Not lost, just confused.

It was the difference between not and being able
to find one's way out or back.
He went to get her a blanket from the car
and thought of maps, and all his strategies
to find her.

Starlings were a noisy crowd behind them,
a wake for summer.
She laughed kindly at his image,
leaned on his shoulder. Both of his arms
went around her.

In the middle distance a Blue Heron's vague alteration,
a small distraction he decided against.

—I don't want to sound too much like a lover
but it was always fine
to hold you.

She was leaving in the morning.
—You're easy to be with
but the coming to you is hard.
A memory came to him, a memory from before
he could remember his age.

Taken to a pasture past woods and streams
far back on the farm, he'd been told
to drive the cows to the distant barn,
that if he kept them moving,
they'd lead the way.

She put more pressure on his arms. Water sounded
on the pilings like the hoofs of fording cows,
tree shadows like bovine silhouettes,
territory hard to find his way alone in,
not lost, but losing.